A Promise Kept

A PROMISE KEPT

Robertson McQuilkin

Tyndale House Publishers, Inc.   Wheaton, Illinois

Dedicated to those Muriel loved
almost as much as she loved me,
the fruit of our love:
Mardi, Bob, David, Jan, Amy, and Kent

CONTENTS

ACKNOWLEDGMENTS

There are strong reasons this story should never have been told.

I'm a private person by nature. To write and speak about our story—Muriel's and mine—has come only after repeated requests and gentle pressure from friends. One further motivation: Following the publication of the first article, "Living by Vows" (*Christianity Today*, October 8, 1990), the response convinced me that God could use the story to help some of his people. So, reluctantly, I write again.

Yet that very response leads to another problem. Why should people consider my experience special? The world is full of people doing what I do. I feel a twinge of guilt that my story is told and retold rather than theirs. Besides, there are so many who carry far greater loads, and that with quiet heroism. I would rather their song be sung.

Another real hesitancy is that some might get the impression that I'm advocating my approach to caring for a loved one as the only right approach. And that misperception could easily bring condemnation or guilt for the many who cannot, because of various circumstances, do as I have done. I hope none will hear me advocating my approach as the only or best approach in all circumstances. I'm just telling my story, celebrating the joys of married love, not pushing a specific agenda for caregiving.

Yet in spite of all the hazards, I've been persuaded to share a small part of our story with the prayer that some may find encouragement.

Many have helped in the telling, too many to name. But still I'm indebted and grateful. I would be remiss, however, if I did not mention the editors of Christianity Today and Word of Life Press, Japan, without whose encouragement I would not have written at all. Some of the material used in preparing this book appeared originally in Christianity Today as "Living by Vows" (October 8, 1990), and "Muriel's Blessing" (February 5, 1996), and in the book In Sickness or in Health, (Word of Life Press, Tokyo, 1996).

Though all the stories in this book are true, a few of the names of people have been altered to protect their privacy.

In Sickness and in Health

WE WERE VISITING FRIENDS IN FLORIDA THE SUMMER OF 1978 WHEN MURIEL, MY WIFE, STARTED TO REPEAT THE SAME STORY SHE had told us five minutes earlier. I reminded her that this was a rerun. She just laughed and continued. *Funny,* I thought, *that's never happened before.* But it happened again. Occasionally. She was fifty-five years old.

Three years later, when she was hospitalized to check out her heart, a young doctor called me to one side and said, "You may need to think about the possibility of Alzheimer's." I was incredulous. *These young doctors are so presumptuous. And insensitive.* Muriel could do almost anything she had ever done. True, we had stopped entertaining in our home—no small loss for the president of a thriving seminary and Bible college. Though she was a great cook and hostess, it had become increasingly difficult to plan a menu. But Alzheimer's? I had hardly heard the name. Still, a dread began to lurk around the fringes of my consciousness.

When her memory deteriorated further, we went to a neurologist friend who gave her the full battery of tests and, by elimination, diagnosed her as having Alzheimer's. But there was some question in my mind since she had none of the typical physical deterioration. So we went to the Duke University Medical Center, believing we should get the best available second opinion. My heart sank as the doctor asked her to name the Gospels and she looked pleadingly at me for help. But she quickly bounced back and laughed at herself. A little nervous, perhaps, but nothing was going to get *her* down!

We were urged by friends—on average, once a week—to pursue every variety of treatment: vitamins, exorcism, chemicals, this guru, that healer, the other clinic. Each suggestion was an expression of love, but how could I even check them all out, let alone pursue them? We chose to accept the verdict and not chase around the country after every new miracle treatment we might hear about. Go standard. We would trust the Lord to work a miracle in Muriel if he so desired or work a miracle in me if he didn't.

So this is it

Multitudes in this fallen world bravely bear far greater burdens than mine.

Some of them are on my special prayer list—a dear friend whose daughter, with drug-numbed mind, is in and out of mental wards, in and out of bed with anyone and everyone. Year after dreadful year. Whose baby is she carrying now? Or the couple in deadly combat; the love they once knew, dead. Those with children who steadfastly refuse the knowledge of God. As I felt the pain of my friends, my own did not seem so severe. Still, there were moments. . . .

The radio-station manager, the program manager, and the producer of my wife's morning program, *Looking Up*, asked for an appointment. I knew that occasionally a program she produced was not used, but the response to her monologue of upbeat encouragement continued to be strong. In fact, though the program was designed for women, businessmen often told me how they arranged their morning affairs so they could listen too. As the appointment began, the three executives seemed uneasy. After a few false starts, I caught the drift. They were reluctantly letting me know that an era was ending. Only months before, they had talked of national syndication.

"Are you meeting with me to let us know that Muriel cannot continue?" I asked, trying to help them out. They seemed relieved that their painful message was out and none of them had to say it. *So this is it,* I thought. *Her public ministry is over.* No more conferences, TV, radio. I should have guessed the time had come.

But she didn't think so! She may have lost the radio program, but she insisted on accepting invitations to speak, even though invariably she would come home crushed and bewildered that her train of thought was lost and things did not go well. Gradually, reluctantly, she gave up public ministry.

Still she could counsel the many young people who sought her out, she could drive and shop, write her children. The letters didn't always make good sense, but then, the children would say, "Mom always was a bit spacey."

She volunteered to read textbooks for a blind graduate student. The plan was to put them on tape so that others could use them. I was puzzled that those responsible never used the tapes, till it began to dawn on me that reading and writing were following art and public speaking in slowly slipping out of reach. She was disappointed with each failure and frustration, but only momentarily. Then she would laugh and have another go at it.

Muriel never knew what was happening to her, though occasionally when there was a reference to Alzheimer's on TV she would muse aloud, "I wonder if I'll ever have that?" It didn't

seem painful for her, but it was a slow dying for me to watch the vibrant, creative, articulate person I knew and loved gradually dimming out.

Scary Business

As I plowed full speed ahead in life and ministry, the first warning shot across the bow of my ship was a call on the pulpit phone in a church in distant Pennsylvania. (I had always wondered what those phones were for!) It was almost time for me to speak when the emergency call came through: Muriel feared she was having a heart attack. It turned out that there was nothing wrong with her heart, but something had gone very wrong with my leaving her alone. Muriel began to travel with me more often.

Memory loss is scary business. *Where am I? How can I get home? Where is my husband, my only security?* When traveling with me, Muriel never panicked. If we were separated, she'd strike out with her customary cheerful confidence and find her way out of the labyrinthine tangle of misperceptions.

In 1986 we were on a wide-ranging ministry tour and Muriel stayed close to me in our trek through Pakistan, the Philippines, and Taiwan, reveling in every exotic sight and experience.

"You've given me such an exciting life!" she often exulted.

Then came Tokyo, largest and most complicated of cities. I left her in our room while I ran a brief errand. On my return, Muriel was gone! My heart sank—how could I ever find her in the unending maze of narrow, winding streetlets? I ran—something an adult does not do in Japan—first down one street, then another. I asked at a police box, I asked shopkeepers, I asked passersby. She couldn't have gone far in so short a time, and certainly not unnoticed.

When I finally arrived back at the mission headquarters where we were staying, a sense of panic had begun to rise. Lest it engulf my spirit, with only half-concealed desperation I asked the mission executives to pray with me. As we prayed we heard that familiar burst of laughter that often heralded Muriel's arrival. Oblivious to the panic

she had set off, she bubbled over with an exciting story of adventure. She had gone to find me but instead had discovered a school yard full of delightful children to watch and "talk" to. Then a nice teacher called a taxi to bring her home. Home? How did the "nice taxi man" know where "home" was? Seems he stopped at the same police box I had alerted shortly before. . . .

I changed tactics once again, trying to keep pace with the ever-shifting boundaries of safety. A few months later, we found ourselves in a motel room on the lovely beach of Grand Cayman Island. I had learned my lesson in Tokyo—never let Muriel out of my sight. She played on the beach in front of our motel, building sand castles. I could see in her work evidences of the skilled artist that once was. From the desk where I was preparing my messages, I kept watch. She reminded me, sitting there in the sand, of one of our three-year-olds in an earlier, carefree day.

Then suddenly, incredibly, she was gone!

I ran down the beach one direction, realizing that with every step she could be getting farther down the beach the other way.

Finally, exhausted and helpless, I returned to our room—only to discover Muriel! Seems some "nice young man" had offered her a ride home. He drove down the beach highway till she spotted our motel. Spotted our motel? In that string of look-alikes even I had difficulty spotting ours. I believe in guardian angels. In younger days, our children claimed that "God hasn't given Mom a guardian angel. He's assigned a whole platoon to her!" Such was the delightful flitting butterfly I had captured for my own.

$\mathcal{R}$ESTLESS FEET

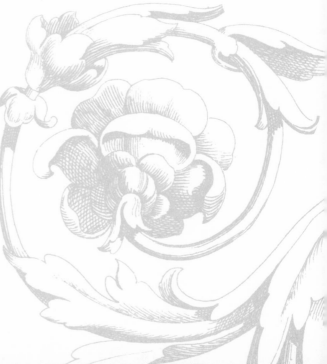

Before long, Muriel began to wander away from our home on campus. A young woman named Sandi came to live with us and be a companion to Muriel. She didn't last long. Muriel, such a self- starting, free-spirited, nonstop doer, became fearful and agitated the moment I left home, felt trapped when she wasn't free to follow me, and "escaped" daily. Many times a day!

To help alleviate Muriel's fears and Sandi's frustrations, I called often from the office and daily when on the road. Except from Tanzania. There it took most of the day waiting at a dusty outpost, miles from the school at which I was speaking, to get through to South Carolina. When at last the connection was made, Sandi was beside herself. Muriel was incorrigible — I must come home immediately.

Though cooler heads prevailed and Sandi was finally persuaded to let me finish my assignment, she had had it. The moment I arrived she resigned, and no amount of assurance that Muriel would henceforth accompany me on every out-of-town trip could dissuade her. Muriel, however, was delighted with the new plan to travel with me always.

A gifted artist, Muriel had long dreamed of going to London, the city she considered the art capital of the world. Britannia not only ruled the waves, it seems; Britannia also plundered the art treasure troves of the world! So when I received an opportunity to minister in England, we stayed in London for over a week. But we were too late.

With high anticipation, I found the Tate gallery with the world's largest collection of Muriel's favorite artist, Turner. A great sadness swept over me as I watched her rush through the gallery with never a glance at the masterworks she had loved so long. So, keeping pace with those restless feet, we spent our time flitting about the great city, occasionally lighting for a moment to enjoy the grandeur. When we reached the Parliament, Muriel wanted to follow the crowd into the building. I knew she could never survive the long wait in that line, so we walked on, taking pictures of the antiquity that surrounded us.

I focused on a statue of some important personage, and when I turned to walk on, Muriel was not in sight. I dashed to a nearby bobby, standing imperturbably on guard.

On guard for what? Certainly not for a wandering gray-haired American woman! He was totally indifferent to my plight. Maybe she had joined the queue of Parliament wanna-bes, I thought. As I ran alongside the line of patiently waiting tourists, suddenly, from the door through which some of them periodically entered, emerged a uniformed young lady escorting gate-crasher Muriel. There was no exciting story of meeting the prime minister, though, just a subdued grumbling about this not-so-nice young lady who had stopped her midcourse.

To Love and to Cherish

CARE OF MURIEL WAS NOT ONLY CHALLENGING WHEN WE REACHED OUR DESTINATION, IT WAS EQUALLY CHALLENGING EN ROUTE. I BEGAN to empathize with those young fathers you sometimes see in an airport, accosting perfect strangers who emerge from the women's restroom, "Did you see a little six-year-old girl in there?" Airline attendants watched in well-guarded bemusement as I crowded with Muriel into the tiny cubicle that houses the in-flight toilet. I knew what they didn't; if she ever got the door shut—unlikely as that might be—she never could have gotten it open again.

Once our flight was delayed in Atlanta and we had to wait a couple of hours. Now that's a challenge. Every few minutes, the same questions, the same answers about what we're doing here, when are we going home? And every few minutes we'd take a fast-paced walk down the terminal in earnest search of—what? Muriel had always been a speed walker. I had to jog to keep up with her!

An attractive woman executive type sat across from us, working diligently on her computer. Once, when we returned from an excursion, she said something, without looking up from her papers. Since no one else was nearby I assumed she had spoken to me or at least mumbled in protest of our constant activity.

"Pardon?" I asked.

"Oh," she said, "I was just asking myself, 'Will I ever find a man to love me like that?'"

SACRIFICES

For years I struggled with the question of whether ministry or Muriel should be sacrificed. Should I put the kingdom of God first and, for the sake of Christ and the kingdom, arrange for institutionalization?

Trusted, lifelong friends—wise and godly—urged me to do this. "Muriel would become accustomed to the new environment quickly."

Would she? Would anyone love her at all, let alone love her as I do? Would she not miss that love? I had often seen the empty, listless faces of those lined up in wheelchairs along the corridors of such places, waiting, waiting for the fleeting visit of some loved one. In such an environment, Muriel would be tamed only by drugs or bodily restraints, of that I was confident.

People who do not know me well have said, "Well, you always said, 'God first, family second, ministry third.'" But I never said that. To put God first means that all the responsibilities he gives are first too. Yet sorting out responsibilities that seem to conflict is tricky business.

Eventually, I approached the board of trustees with the need to begin the search for my successor. I told them that when Muriel needed me full-time, she would have me.

When the time came, the decision was firm and it didn't take any heavy-duty calculation. Soon after the decision was announced I wrote a letter to our constituency:

Twenty-two years is a long time. But then again, it can be shorter than one anticipates. And how do you say good-bye to friends you do not wish to leave?

The decision to come to Columbia was the most difficult I have had to make; the decision to leave 22 years later, though painful, was one of the easiest. It was almost as if God engineered the circumstances so that I had no alternatives. Let me explain.

My dear wife, Muriel, has been in failing mental health for about 12 years. So far I have been able to carry both her ever-growing needs and my leadership responsibility at Columbia. But recently it has become apparent that Muriel is contented most of the time she is with me and almost none of the time I am away from her. It is not just "discontent." She is filled with fear—even terror—that she has lost me and always goes in search of me when I leave home. So it is clear to me that she needs me now, full-time.

Perhaps it would help you understand if I shared with you what I shared in chapel at the time of the announcement of my resignation. The decision was made, in a way, 42 years ago when I promised to care for Muriel "in sickness and in health . . . till death do us part." So, as I told the students and faculty, as a man of my word, integrity has something to do with it. But so does fairness. She has cared for me fully and sacrificially all these years; if I cared for her for the next 40 years I would not be out of her debt. Duty, however, can be grim and stoic. But there is more: I love Muriel. She is a

delight to me — her childlike dependence and confidence in me, her warm love, occasional flashes of that wit I used to relish so, her happy spirit and tough resilience in the face of her continual distressing frustration. I don't *have* to care for her. I *get* to! It is a high honor to care for so wonderful a person.

I have been startled by the response to the announcement of my resignation. Husbands and wives renewing marriage vows, pastors telling the story to their people. It was a mystery to me, until a distinguished oncologist, who lives constantly with dying people, told me, "Almost all women stand by their men; very few men stand by their women." Perhaps people sensed this contemporary tragedy and somehow were helped by a simple choice I considered the only option.

It's more than keeping promises and being fair, however. As I watch her brave descent into oblivion, Muriel is the joy of my life. Daily I discern new manifestations of the kind of person she is, the wife I always loved.

A GIFT OF LOVE

Muriel picked flowers outside—
anyone's—and filled the house with
them. Then she began to pick them
inside, too. Someone had given us
a beautiful Easter lily, two stems with
four or five lilies on each and more to
come. One day I came into the kitchen
and there on the windowsill over the sink
was a vase with a stem of lilies in it. I learned to "go with
the flow" and not correct irrational behavior. After all, it is just
that—irrational. She meant no harm and didn't understand what
should be done, nor would she remember a rebuke. Nevertheless, I
did the irrational too—I told her how disappointed I was, how the
lilies would soon die, the buds would never bloom, and *please* do not
break off the other stem.

The next day I told our youngest son, Kent, of my stupid
rebuke of his mother and how bad I felt about it. As we sat on the
porch swing, his mother came to the door with a gift of love for

me—she carefully laid the other stem of lilies on the table with a gentle smile and turned back into the house.

I said simply, "Thank you."

Kent said, "You're doing better, Dad!"

On one occasion, the dentist needed to have Muriel open and shut her mouth often to test a new crown. But when he said, "Please open," she clenched her teeth. The more he pled with her, the tighter she clenched. I tried, too, but to no avail. She knew she wasn't pleasing us, so she tried harder. Tears welled up in my eyes as I saw the intensity of her concentration, the fear in her eyes— how she wanted to please. But she had gotten it all backward. I love her so.

And Muriel loved me, too. By then she couldn't speak in sentences, only words—and often words that didn't make sense. *No* when she meant *yes*, for example. But she could still say one sentence. And she said it often: "I love you."

She not only said it, she acted it. During the latter years of my presidency at Columbia, it became increasingly difficult to keep her at home. As soon as I left for the office, she would take out after me. With me, she was content; without me she was distressed, sometimes terror-stricken.

The walk to school is a mile round-trip. She would make that trip as many as ten times a day—*ten miles,* speed walking. Sometimes at night when I helped her undress, I found bloody feet. When I told our family doctor, he choked up. "Such love," he said simply. Then, after a moment, "I have a theory that the characteristics developed across the years come out at times like these."

For Better, for Worse

RIENDS AND FAMILY OFTEN ASK, "HOW ARE YOU DOING?" MEANING, I TAKE IT, "HOW DO YOU FEEL?" I AM AT A LOSS HOW TO respond. There is that subterranean grief that won't go away. It increases daily as the lights go out. I would be just as alone if I had never known her as she once was, but the loneliness of the night hours is because I did know her. Do I grieve for her loss or mine?

Further, there is sorrow that it is increasingly difficult to meet her needs. Yet I guess friends are asking, not about *her* needs, but about mine. Or perhaps they wonder, in the contemporary jargon, how I am "coping," as they reflect on how the reputedly indispensable characteristics of a good marriage have slipped away, one by one.

A letter to a national columnist read, "I ended the relationship because it wasn't meeting my needs."

The counselor's response was predictable: "What were your needs that didn't get met by her in the relationship? Do you still have these same needs? What would she have to do to fill these needs? Could she do it?" Needs for communication, understanding, affirmation, common interests, sexual fulfillment—the list goes on. If the needs are not met, split. He offered no alternatives.

There is an eerie irrelevance to every one of those criteria for me.

I used to have long lists of "coping strategies," which had to be changed weekly, sometimes daily. Grocery shopping together may once have been fun recreation, but not so fun when she begins to load other people's carts and make off with them, disappearing down an aisle into the vast labyrinth we call a supermarket. I've repented of those years of poking fun at "woman talk" as I diligently inquire of a hostess about recipes and call lady friends to learn what kind of shampoo works best after a permanent. How do you get a person to eat or take a bath when she steadfastly refuses?

DISCOVERIES

As Alzheimer's slowly locked away one part of my Muriel, then another, every loss for her shut down a part of me. Ministry was changing, of course, from less public to more private. There was another sense of loss, however, an unassuageable ache deep inside, as I watched my vivacious companion of the years slip from me.

Even in this loss, however, I made a wonderful discovery. As Muriel became ever more dependent on me, our love seeped to deeper, unknown crevices of the heart. Though she never knew what was happening to her, as I cared for her she responded with gratitude and cheerful contentment. It was no great effort to do the loving thing for one who was altogether lovable. My imprisonment turned out to be a delightful liberation to love more fully than I had ever known. We found the chains of confining circumstance to be, not instruments of torture, but bonds to hold us closer.

But there was even greater liberation. It has to do with

God's love. No one ever needed me like Muriel, and no one ever responded to my efforts so totally as she. It's the nearest thing I've experienced on a human plane to what my relationship with God was designed to be: God's unfailing love poured out in constant care of helpless me. Surely he planned that relationship to draw from me the kind of love and gratitude Muriel had for her man. Her insatiable — even desperate — longing to be with me, her quiet confidence in my ability and desire to care for her, a mirror reflection of what my love for God should be.

That was the first discovery — the power of love to liberate in the very bondage imposed by unwanted circumstances. People don't always understand that.

But I made another discovery as well, quite the opposite: broken shackles can turn out to be an imprisonment. Here's the way I found out. The response to two articles in which I shared some of our story caught me by surprise. Somehow the story seemed to resonate with all sorts of people — those who have a suffering loved one, those who fear for their own future, those who find an affirmation of their own love stories. But there's a darker side. I've received dozens of visits and agonizing letters from women whose husbands have broken the shackles of marriage, from men whose wives have broken free and left both lives in shambles.

Ours is a day of passionate pursuit of self-fulfillment. And the folk wisdom of twentieth-century America holds that fulfillment can be found only in freedom. So, if some responsibility or commitment, some relationship or value shackles, you have a moral obligation to yourself to break free.

But it's a fantasy. That doorway to freedom and

fulfillment may turn out to be the doorway to a stronger imprisonment. I've watched in sadness as many friends and acquaintances march through that doorway. The new bondage may be subterranean, below the level of consciousness even. But such a person has broken one set of shackles only to shut herself or himself off from the soaring freedom of experiencing God's highest and best. He who preserves his life, affirming himself, will lose it all, said Jesus. Only the one who says no to self-interest for Christ and the gospel cause can ever find the treasure of true life—freedom and fulfillment in Christ. But we don't seem to get it.

Two young couples approached me one day. Seems the women had read my story "Living by Vows," wept appropriately, and cajoled their husbands into reading it. When they had read it, each wife had asked her husband the same question: "Would you do that for me?" And each husband, independently from the other, had responded: "Don't put me on the spot!" The two husbands, standing by as this story was told, grinned sheepishly. I wouldn't worry about such young-marriage banter except that I've heard it so often. And I've seen the end of the story too.

For months a friend had been counseling a couple whose marriage was in shambles. The wife had seen a lawyer, was pursuing divorce. Our mutual friend had given them a copy of "Living by Vows." When she read it, that broken woman had sobbed, "Oh, if only my George had loved me like that, things would be so different." When she finally filed for divorce, she put it more formally: "Long ago . . . George, in effect, abandoned our marriage. He chose his priorities, and I have not been one of them." Both partners, in struggling to be free, had worked themselves into ever deeper bondage: broken hearts, broken home, broken church, a ministry permanently hobbled.

Of course, it's not just the shackles of an unfulfilling marriage. I hear constantly about those who have refused to assume responsibility for a handicapped loved one, or who fulfill an obligation with such resentment that both caregiver and care

receiver are mired in misery. And every story fills me with sadness, for it need not be so. Bondage can be a delightful liberation.

ℒIFE IS SIMPLER, NOW

Muriel was increasingly my ministry, and I delighted in it. Reflecting on how four decades of love-intoxicated life together were coming to a close, I put it in a bit of verse for her, words she might never really understand, but, I hope, a love she would ever feel:

Life is simpler, now.
Time and tide have set
The boundaries of choice:
Is it to stop
And wait
The gathering storm,
Hand in hand?
Or should we merely
Slow the pace
And press ahead,
Your painful sacrifice

Enabling me to strike
A few more blows?

Life is simpler, now,
Defined no longer
By what we do
So much as who we are:
I am your security,
My companionship
Your only haven
From the buffeting of

Strange winds
Deeply felt
And little understood;
I am set to shield you
From those grim terrors
That may lurk around the
        bend.
And you?
Your mind is tethered
By strands of love
And joy and tough
        endurance,
Woven strong across the
        years.
I stand in awe.
And take courage
From your strength
        To press on.

Life is simpler now,
No longer knitting these two
        lives
With threads of conversation,
But with the wordless
Assurances of love.
The motions of my soul
More deeply tender,

Hammered by the blows
Of adverse winds.
Love more pure, intense,
Emerges from the fire.

Life is simpler, now —
God's good gift
For two busy people
Who celebrate the past
And quietly wait
With hope.

From This Day Forward

ONE YOUNG WIFE, STRUGGLING WITH ENTRAP-MENT IN WHAT SHE CONSIDERED A BAD MARRIAGE, SAID OF MY ATTITUDE TOWARD Muriel, "That's not reasonable."

Most folks are too courteous to say so, but some seem to wonder, "Are you for real, or are you some kind of freak?" So let me tell you someone else's story—Jerry's.

He met me at the airport. We had been friends for years—a friendship I cherished, not least because he was a deeply spiritual and powerfully gifted man of God. But Jerry was troubled. So troubled, in fact, that he immediately steered me to a table in a stairwell of the terminal so we could talk. He was distressed because something was happening to Betty, his wife, and he didn't know what to do. I'd never seen him like that before—not knowing what to do. He was struggling, trying not to accept the fact that there were symptoms of Alzheimer's disease. Maybe I could help.

"Does the church know about it?"

"Oh no, I've not shared these fears with anyone."

"What do your children think?"

"I haven't told them." In loyalty to his wife, he didn't want to expose her to what others might think, especially since he was himself so uncertain as to what was happening.

That weekend I stayed in a home that was tense, confused, and verging on desperation. I was incredulous—theirs had been a home of beautiful Christian grace unfailing. But now Jerry constantly corrected Betty: "No, you haven't served the muffins, yet . . . no, we didn't get those in New England, we got them in Canada . . . no, those aren't the eggs that will break. . . ." Betty, for her part, was quietly seething. She called me aside to tell me terrible things about her husband. They were imagined, but those imaginations tormented her day and night. Betty was out of reach, of course, but I told Jerry he

must change, affirm his beloved, stop correcting her, and no, there was no use trying to keep it from the congregation. They already knew something was up, I assured him, and they would embrace him and Betty with loving care if he'd just come out of hiding. Especially, stop trying to correct her. It's only going to get worse.

"But, Robertson," he said, "it's going to be very hard to ignore it when Betty is just plain wrong. All my life, I've stood for truth." Another reason he explained months later: "It pains me so to see her slipping away from reality. I want to hold her to it."

I tried to encourage them both, but it looked pretty grim. A few weeks later, however, Betty finally agreed to see a neurologist. When she heard the verdict, an astounding transformation took place. If that's what it is, we'll just see it through together, she concluded. How would they let the congregation know? Jerry suggested that Betty be the one to tell them, and after some persuading, she agreed. The next Sunday morning, she stood before the large congregation and told them what God was up to in her life.

I visited in their home a few months later and could hardly believe the change. They were like newlyweds. Betty was more confused than ever, but Jerry didn't try to correct her. "It's nearly killing me to change my whole approach to life," he said.

And Betty confided in me that her man was the most loving, caring, understanding husband in the world.

Often she would find refuge at her piano—and what a musician she had been! One evening, as I came into the living room, Betty was singing again in that lovely contralto voice. I wept as she sang:

*"I cannot see beyond the moment, tomorrow's strength
　　comes not today;
But, blessed Lord, I trust Thy keeping for just
　　the next step of my way.
Lord Jesus, keep my next step faithful to paths
　　marked out by God for me!
Hold Thou me up, O mighty Savior! My strength
　　and hope are all in Thee.*

"*The storms that gather 'round my pathway may hide the next*
   step from my sight,
But faith can walk with God in darkness, and He will guide
   that step aright.
Lord Jesus, keep my next step faithful to paths marked out by
   God for me!
Hold Thou me up, O mighty Savior! My strength and hope
   are all in Thee."

Unexpectedly, Jerry came in and found me thus deeply moved. We embraced and wept together as he told me he and Betty had never known such love, such tenderness. How she needed him! How she trusted him! And how he loved her. . . . He said he

couldn't explain it, but they found themselves often telling one another of that love in words they'd never heard before. In fact, as she slipped further into Alzheimer's, Betty told him she was so glad for her illness because of the love it had unleashed in their lives. "I would never change it," she said.

They, too, were liberated by the power of a mighty love.

ℛEAL LOVE

Once I completely lost it. In the days when Muriel could still stand and walk and we had not resorted to diapers, sometimes there were "accidents." I was on my knees beside her, trying to clean up the mess as she stood, confused, by the toilet. It would have been easier if she weren't so insistent on helping. I got more and more frustrated. Suddenly, to make her stand still, I slapped her calf, as if that would do any good. It wasn't a hard slap, but she was startled. I was too. Never in over forty years of marriage had I ever so much as touched her in anger or in rebuke of any kind. Never. I had never even been tempted, in fact.

But now, when she needed me most. . . .

Sobbing, I pled with her to forgive me—no matter that she didn't understand words any better than she could speak them. So I turned to the Lord to tell him how sorry I was. It took me days to get over it. Maybe God bottled those tears to quench the fires that might ignite again someday.

It wasn't long till I found myself in the same condition, on the floor in the bathroom. Muriel wanted to help—hadn't cleaning up messes been her specialty? But now those busy hands didn't know exactly what to do. I mopped frantically, trying to fend off the interfering hands, and contemplated how best to get a soiled slip over a head that was totally opposed to the idea. At that moment Chuck Swindoll boomed from the radio in the kitchen, "Men! Are you at home? *Really* at home?" In the midst of my stinking immersion I smiled. "Yeah, Chuck, I really am." Do I ever wish I weren't?

Recently a student wife asked, "Don't you ever get tired?"

"Tired? Every night. That's why I go to bed."

"No, I mean tired of . . ." and she tilted her head toward Muriel, who sat silently in her wheelchair, her vacant eyes saying, "No one at home just now."

"Why, no, I don't get tired," I responded. "I love to care for her. She's my precious."

"Well, I certainly would."

And she would. In fact, she does. In a marriage young and bubbling with romance, two handsome, healthy, smart people with big dreams. . . . But, as she told me, a person can get tired of always affirming a mate, especially when there is so little to commend. Shouldn't love make a difference?

Love is said to evaporate if it's not mutual, if the other person doesn't communicate, if they don't carry their share of the load, if it's not physical. When I hear the litany of essentials for a happy marriage, I count off what my beloved can no longer contribute and contemplate how truly mysterious love is. I was preparing dinner recently when the voice of a renowned radio preacher announced something that startled me. He said an authoritative study indicated that when terminal illness strikes a mate, seven out of ten American spouses split. And since husbands leave home far more frequently than wives in such circumstances, what must the numbers be for them? Nine out of ten? Just when they're needed most. . . . I thought to myself, *How could they do such a thing?* Maybe they're having a love affair. With themselves. Indeed, love is a mysterious thing.

The five-column headline read **Love Helps Alzheimer's Victims Survive, Study Says.** The reporter wrote: "What's love got to do with it? Just about everything, says a researcher who studied what happens in a marriage when a spouse gets Alzheimer's disease."

I was there when Dr. Lore Wright gave that report. In her study of forty-seven couples over a two-year period, she predicted with 100 percent accuracy who would die, based on her analysis of the love relationship between husband and wife.

I attended a workshop in which another expert told us that there were two reasons people keep a family member at home rather than in a nursing facility: economic necessity or feelings of guilt. Afterward I spoke with her privately, trying to elicit some other possible motive for keeping someone at home. But she insisted those were the only two motives.

Finally I asked, "What about love?"

"Oh," she replied, "we put that under guilt."

So much for love!

For Richer, for Poorer

LOVING MURIEL ISN'T HARD; SHE'S SO LOVABLE. BUT WHAT ABOUT MY OTHER LOVES? LIKE MY FORMER WORK?

"Do you miss being president?" asked Steve, a freshman, as we sat in our little garden.

I told him I'd never thought about it, but, on reflection, no. Exciting, exhilarating, significant as my work had been, I didn't miss it. I enjoyed learning to cook and keep house, I said, and making this garden. The garden business was a little late. Muriel always wanted a Japanese garden, but I never got around to it, so now it's sort of a memorial to lost dreams, I guess. And I enjoy preaching around the country on weekends and writing articles and books in the quiet hours. No, I never looked back.

But that night I reflected on his question. Finally I turned to the Lord. "Father, it's OK. I like this assignment and I have no regrets. But something has occurred to me. If the Coach puts a man on the bench, he must not want him in the game. You needn't tell me, of course, but if you'd like to let me in on the secret, I'd like to know—why don't you need me in the game?"

I didn't sleep well that night and awoke contemplating the puzzle. Muriel was still mobile at that time, so we set out on our morning walk around the block. She wasn't too sure on her feet, so we went slowly and held hands. We live in what is euphemistically called a transitional neighborhood, where the sidewalks are often peopled with those who've lived hard and, it would seem, outlived hope.

A short stretch of sidewalk is bordered by a weedy embankment on the left and a very busy thoroughfare on the right. I was grateful we never met anyone there because someone would have to get out into the traffic. But this day I heard footsteps behind me and looked back to see the familiar form of a local derelict weaving his way behind us. I thought, *He'll never catch up.* But he did and, without missing a step, staggered out into the road and back up to the sidewalk in front of us.

There he turned, looked us up and down, and said, "Tha's good. I likes 'at. Tha's *real* good. I likes it." Then he headed off down the street, mumbling to himself over and over, "Tha's good. I likes it."

I enjoyed the moment with a chuckle, grateful for the affirmation.

When we reached our little garden and sat down, his words came back to me. I was startled. "Lord, could you speak through the mouth of a half-inebriated old derelict?" I wondered aloud. Then the realization hit me, *You could and you did! It is you who are whispering to my spirit, "I like it, it's good. . . ."* *I may be on the bench, but if you like it and say it's good, that's all that counts.*

$\mathcal{T}$HE SECRET

"What are your resources?" the TV interviewer asked.

I hadn't thought about it; but now I have. Praise helps. For example, I think my life must be happier than 95 percent of the people on planet earth—sins forgiven, the smile of God, a home filled with laughter and contentment. Why, people with good sense often miss out on that! Muriel's a joy to me; life is good to both of us, in different ways. But I'm thinking of something more basic than just "counting your blessings."

In 1992 the blows of life had left me numb— my dearest on earth slipping from me, my eldest son snatched away in a tragic accident, my life's work abandoned at its peak. Oh, I didn't hold it against God, but my faith could better be described as resignation. The joy had drained away; the passion in my love for God had frozen over. I knew I was in trouble. If the only Companion you have in the lonely hours grows distant. . . .

Of course, the passion of his love for me never cooled. Even in the darkest hours, when I felt my grip slipping and I was in danger of sliding into the abyss of doubt, what always caught and held me was the vision of God's best-loved, pinioned in criminal execution in my place. How could someone who loved me that much let anything hurt me without cause? But still, a one-sided love affair isn't very satisfactory. I missed the intimate companionship.

Then I remembered the secret I'd learned in younger days — I went away to a mountain hideaway to be alone with God. There, though it was slow coming, I gradually was able to break free from preoccupation with my troubles and concentrate on Jesus. When that happened, I relearned what God had taught me more than once before: *The heavy heart lifts on the wings of praise.*

There are other resources. Family. Not my children, for though they love us dearly, they're scattered from Wisconsin to Japan to the slums of Calcutta. Sometimes I'm tempted to envy the life of those friends whose children and grandchildren are gathered close for daily support. But my sisters, one by one, have retired and moved back to Columbia from the ends of the earth. They care for us lovingly. And friends do too. It won't do to cultivate friends for the payback—that's not true friendship. But I've concluded that those who don't build friendships in the spring and summer of life must find winter a lonely time.

Memories help too. Muriel stocked the cupboard of my mind with the best of them. I often live again a special moment of love she planned so creatively or laugh at some remembered outburst of her irrepressible approach to life. Sometimes the happy doesn't bubble up with joy, but rains down gently with tears. When Joy Gresham reminded C. S. Lewis that their joy would soon end, that she would die, he replied that he didn't want to think about that. Joy responded, "The pain is part of the happiness. That's the deal."

It's true. In the summer of '95 Muriel's right hand went limp — the first major decline since she lost the ability to stand and to feed herself eighteen months before. A little loss, you would think, but I shed a few tears. It's almost like part of me dies with each of her little deaths. That precious hand, so creative, so loving, so busy for me and everyone else. But it wasn't just the old memories. That right hand was the last way she had to communicate. She would reach out to hold hands, pat me on the back when I hugged her, push me away when she didn't like what I was doing. I missed her hand. Memories, sweet and bittersweet.

My VALENTINE

I often remember Muriel's repartee. I once remonstrated that she didn't know everything. "I don't know everything?" she shot

back. "Why, I know *more* than everything. I know some things that aren't so!"

Once, in reply to her request to do something, I said I was already doing something else. "Well, it's a poor man that can't do two things at once," she said. Muriel, being a woman, could do three things at once, of course, which she consistently did. And with excellence. But not always.

"I'm a selective quitter," she'd announce and cheerfully abandon a project. "If it's worth doing, it's worth doing well? Pshaw. Very few things in this life are worth doing well."

Once, before we signed off for sleep, I was winning an argument with irresistible logic when she raised up on one elbow, transfixed me with fire in her gray-green eyes, and said, "Well, let me tell you something. Logic's not everything, and feeling's not nothing." In the uninterrupted silences of today, the memories of sweet and spicy talk long gone bring pleasure once again.

It's just as well I have those memories of past conversations, for she hasn't spoken a coherent word in months—years, if you mean a sentence, a conversation—though occasionally she tries,

66

mumbling non-words. Would I never hear that voice again? Her radio fans loved it, and it surely energized my life.

Valentine's Day was always special at our house because that was the day in 1948 that Muriel accepted my marriage proposal. On the eve of Valentine's Day in 1995, I read a statement by some specialist that Alzheimer's is the most cruel disease of all, but the victim is actually the caregiver. I wonder why I have never felt like a victim.

A friend wrote, "Muriel doesn't know you anymore, doesn't know anything, really, so it's time to put her in a nursing home and get on with life." The day may come when, because of a change in my health or hers, she could be better cared for by others. But for now she needs me and I need her.

I responded, "Do you realize how lonely I would be without her?"

And neither is Muriel a victim, really. That Valentine's Day eve, as I thought about victimhood, I recalled a time when I was changing her clothes. Instead of the usual scowl reserved for such occasions, she smiled warmly, triggering a happy thought.

"You are one lucky girl," I said. "No wonder you're so contented. You don't have a worry in the world, no fears, no hurt. Everything you need is provided; you're well loved and well cared for. Why, you don't even have any sin to repent of!"

That evening I bathed Muriel on her bed, kissed her good-night (she stills enjoys two things: good food and kissing!), and whispered a prayer over her, "Dear Jesus, you love sweet Muriel more than I, so please keep my beloved through the night; may she hear the angel choirs. . . ."

The next morning I was pedaling on my Exercycle at the foot of her bed and, while Muriel slowly emerged from sleep, I dipped into memories of some of the happy Lovers' Days long gone. Finally she popped awake and, as she often did, smiled at me. Then, for the first time in months, she spoke, calling out to me in a voice clear as a crystal chime, "Love . . . love . . . love . . ."

I jumped from my cycle and ran to embrace her. "Honey, you really do love me, don't you?"

Holding me with her eyes and patting my back, she responded with the only words she could find to express agreement. "I'm nice," she said.

Those may prove to be the last words she ever spoke.

Till Death Do Us Part

MY DAUGHTER, MARDI, GAVE ME A CHRISTMAS GIFT IN 1994, A BIT OF VERSE THAT TELLS MURIEL'S STORY BETTER THAN I EVER COULD.

Wild roses grew in Mother's mind
seeds fell from her hands
and laughter ran
like a mountain brook
out of her heart to water our gardens

she gathered stones and sunlight
moonbeams and melodies
no smallest bit of loveliness
was passed without the sweet caress
of her happy recognition

she gleefully uprooted pretense
and tossed it in the sea
she danced and ran where
others walked

and now the snow falls deep
around the place she spun and shone
scattering God-light from her hair

she goes to visit now
more frequently it seems
her form hangs gently here
we try to care for it and she
comes back sometimes a
     moment
to look out at us
and smiles as if to say
oh yes — you're there — the
     ones I love
but then she wanders back
to stand beside that door
they will not let her enter

and watches angels passing
and listens to the choirs of saints
and whispers softly
may I come in

I still weep when I read those words and sometimes ask, "When will the dawn come?"

CHOICES

"Why don't you let her go?"

I wasn't altogether sure what the lady had in mind by her question, but she didn't leave me long in doubt. The talk-show host in southern California was supposed to interview me about my book *An Introduction to Biblical Ethics,* but he had just read my story "Muriel's Blessing," and that's all he wanted to talk about. Ten minutes into the interview he abruptly announced, "Open line," and I found myself in conversation with an unknown lady on the other side of the continent.

"What do you mean, 'let her go'?" I asked. I thought the talk-show host had made it clear I had let go emotionally. But that isn't what she had in mind.

"Does your wife feed herself?" she asked.

"No . . ."

"Then why don't you stop feeding her? She'd be better off with Jesus, wouldn't she?" I tried to introduce issues about euthanasia, which were outlined in the book we were supposed to be discussing, but the host didn't bite—he left me to the tender mercies of a woman with strong convictions on the subject. After all, "stop feeding her" is what she had done in her own family.

But I would never stop feeding Muriel. Or would I? Actually, that very struggle intensified in my own mind as the day approached, I feared, when Muriel could no longer swallow what I put in her mouth. Should we have a "peg" inserted to put food directly into her stomach? It was a simple procedure, my doctor assured me, and one, of course, we would follow.

But she really would be better off with Jesus, wouldn't she? Though I wouldn't be better off if she were. Was I selfish in wanting to keep her with me? Long ago we had instructed one another never to allow heroic measures or let them plug us into life-sustaining technology when we entered that last irreversible descent to the grave. Why prolong the dying if God beckoned us home? Surely, "to depart, and to be with Christ . . . is far better" (Philippians 1:23). In line with her wishes, then, Muriel was on "no code"—there would be no effort to resuscitate her should her heart or other vital systems shut down. But where does a stomach peg fit in the equation?

I put that question to a friend who lives nearby. Gene was a thoroughly pagan medical professor at the university, so perhaps his

viewpoint might differ from that of my own physician, a godly man and personal friend who loves Muriel and me. But Gene said the same thing. "Of course you'll put in a peg." My dilemma deepened—even if I thought it the right thing and did "let her go," how could I live with myself if the doctors in my life said I should not? And, besides, I wasn't at all sure what "the right thing" was. I asked my children to participate in the decision but none of them responded. Finally, Kent, the youngest, said, "Dad, how can we say anything? It is you who will have to live with the decision after it's all over."

Then came my nephew, a Bible scholar with international standing. Since I seldom saw him, we were catching up on family news and the latest theological hot buttons. Abruptly, Paul changed the subject: "Uncle Robertson, you should not put a stomach peg in Aunt Muriel. It would be wrong. I wish you'd talk with Bob." Bob, Paul's brother, was a surgeon with experience in what he called "a five-minute outpatient procedure under local anesthesia." Not exactly the "heroic measures" we'd long since ruled out. Bob's E-mail flashed back an immediate response to my query: "There's nothing to it. You ought to have it done when Aunt Muriel can no longer swallow food."

But by the time he visited us a few weeks later he had second thoughts. His wife had taken strong exception to his position. Marion loves Muriel dearly and, I suppose, wanted her long wait outside the fast-closed doors of heaven to end. So Bob had asked a colleague, "What would you want me to do if you were in this situation?"

"Oh," said the man, who does the procedure routinely, "I would never want you to put a peg in me." So Bob had begun to waver.

Who am I, then, to be sure? But the agonizing choice is mine, not the doctors' or theologians'.

FINISHING WELL

When will the end come? What form will it take? I don't know. But I still have the confidence that both of us will "get home before dark." That's the prayer I penned on the only personal retreat

Muriel ever took with me. I had often invited her for those annual celebrations with God, but she always had her reasons not to go—the children needed her. But after they had grown and gone, in an unguarded moment she let out the real reason—she was afraid. "What would I pray about for three days? And fasting— I don't think I could hold out." But this time she squelched her apprehensions and went. She had a glorious time with the Lord and with me, but the thing she never tired of telling people ever after was, "God gave Robertson that prayer. He just wrote it down and that was it."

People often ask if I had Muriel in mind when I wrote it; some have even put that conjecture in print! But how could I? It was the summer of 1981, three years after we began our descent into Alzheimer's, to be sure, but two years before we knew what was happening to us. Alzheimer's crept up on us unawares. And yet, shadows had begun to flit around the corners of my mind, and for a brief moment as I reached the last stanza, I did think of Muriel and say, "Lord, if it's to be 'a mind

80

untethered,' please let my precious have 'light fantasies' and not 'grim terrors.'"

Let Me Get Home before Dark

It's sundown, Lord.
The shadows of my life stretch back
into the dimness of the years long spent.
I fear not death, for that grim foe betrays
himself at last, thrusting me forever into life:
Life with you, unsoiled and free.

But I do fear.
I fear the Dark Specter may come too
    soon —
or do I mean too late?
That I should end before I finish or
finish, but not well.
That I should stain your
    honor, shame

your name, grieve your loving heart.
Few, they tell me, finish well. . . .
Lord, let me get home before dark.

The darkness of a spirit
grown mean and small,
fruit shriveled on the vine,
bitter to the taste of my companions,
burden to be borne by those brave few who love me still.
No, Lord. Let the fruit grow lush and sweet,
a joy to all who taste;
Spirit-sign of God at work,
stronger, fuller, brighter at the end.
Lord, let me get home before dark.

The darkness of tattered gifts,
rust-locked, half-spent or ill-spent;
A life that once was used of God now set aside.
Grief for glories gone or
Fretting for a task God never gave.

82

Mourning in the hollow chambers of memory,
Gazing on the faded banners of victories long gone.
Cannot I run well unto the end?
Lord, let me get home before dark.

The outer me decays —
I do not fret or ask reprieve.
The ebbing strength but weans me from
mother earth and grows me up for heaven.
I do not cling to shadows cast by immortality.
I do not patch the scaffold lent to build
the real, eternal me.
I do not clutch about me my cocoon,
vainly struggling to hold hostage
a free spirit pressing to be born.

But will I reach the gate
in lingering pain, body distorted, grotesque?
Or will it be a mind
wandering untethered among light fantasies or

grim terrors?
Of your grace, Father, I humbly ask . . .
Let me get home before dark.

God answered my prayer. When I hear Muriel chuckle quietly in the midnight hour or when her eyes follow me across the room in the morning and our eyes fleetingly connect, the sunshine of that wonderful smile brightens our darkness and I say, "Thank you, Lord. Thank you that it's been 'light fantasies' and not 'grim terrors.' And thank you that we'll get home before dark—both of us."

MY PRECIOUS

Twenty summers ago, Muriel and I began our journey into the twilight. It's midnight now, at least for her. Sometimes I wonder when dawn will break. Even the dread Alzheimer's disease isn't supposed to attack so early and torment so long.

Yet, in her silent world Muriel is so content, so lovable, I sometimes pray, "Please, Lord, could you let me keep her a little longer?" If Jesus took her home, how I would miss her gentle, sweet presence. Oh yes, there are times when I get irritated, but not often. It doesn't make sense. And besides, I love to care for her. She's my precious.

ABOUT THE AUTHOR

Robertson McQuilkin is a homemaker, conference speaker, and writer. He served as president of Columbia Bible College and Seminary (now Columbia International University) from 1968 to 1990. While there, his many responsibilities included teaching ethics and hermeneutics. Prior to assuming duties at Columbia, he and his wife, Muriel, served as missionaries to Japan for twelve years (1956–1968).

Dr. McQuilkin's other books include *An Introduction to Biblical Ethics, Understanding and Applying the Bible, The Great Omission, Free and Fulfilled: Victorious Living in the 21st Century,* and *Life in the Spirit.*